Also by Shiloh, Canine Philosopher

Shilohisms: Worldly Advice from a Chocolate Labrador Retriever

HEAVEN HAS A DOG DOOR

A Dog's Quest to Solve the Greatest Mystery

*A timeless journey
for dog lovers of all ages*

SHILOH
Canine Philosopher

Corner
Spot
Press

Corner
Spot
Press

HEAVEN HAS A DOG DOOR

Shiloh, Canine Philosopher

Copyright © 2025 by Corner Spot Press
Published in the United States by Corner Spot Press
801 S. Broadway, Suite 1
Santa Maria, CA 93454
info@cornerspotpress.com

Library of Congress Control Number: 2025920920

ISBN 979-8-9932593-1-4 (Hardcover – Dust Jacket)
ISBN 979-8-9932593-3-8 (Hardcover – Case Laminate)
ISBN 979-8-9932593-0-7 (Paperback)
ISBN 979-8-9932593-2-1 (eBook)

First Edition, 2025

For Them All

For every dog who has passed through
the eternal Dog Door to Heaven.
May you roam in endless meadows,
bathed in light and peace,
forever free.

Contents

Foreword: The Case for Shiloh

This foreword is drawn from the official record of the Tribunal of Artistic Merit, where Shiloh's authorship was decided.

"Shiloh is a dog. How could she write this book?"

That question came from a dignified man in a suit and tie, referencing Heaven Has a Dog Door, and sitting at a long table with two other committee members. They were at the front of a vintage meeting room where important decisions were made.

Shiloh's very right to be an author was being addressed.

We were appearing before the Tribunal of Artistic Merit, a committee charged with officially considering whether Shiloh could be recognized as an author and canine philosopher.

Shiloh, the Chocolate Labrador Retriever, sat calmly with our staff from Corner Spot Press, her publisher.

As the president of the publishing company, I spoke up.

"You are correct that she is a dog," I said. "Writing, especially typing, is difficult for Shiloh because she only has paws."

The man gave a slight smirk, certain this would be an open and shut case.

"But we worked with her and took our time editing," I continued. "Every idea is hers. Her emotions, her insights, her curiosity. All Shiloh."

He grumbled for a moment, then struck the book in front of him with a rubber stamp.

Approved.

The book slid to the next member, a young professor.

"Dogs cannot be philosophers," she said. "They are not intelligent enough."

Shiloh raised her dogbrows but stayed silent.

I stood. "Humans spend much of their brainpower on work, traffic, and trivial matters. Shiloh's mind is free to focus on loyalty, wonder, and truth without a filter. Add to that her extraordinary senses, and she perceives more of the world than we do. That makes her more than qualified."

The professor smiled and tapped the stamp for approval.

Finally, the last member leaned forward, an older man with a thoughtful face.

"I would like to speak to Shiloh directly. Are you truly a philosopher? And if so, why?"

Shiloh walked deliberately over to the front of the dias and sat before the man. She locked eyes with him.

If you have ever been caught in the stare of a dog that meant the world to you, you know there is a spark, a communication beyond words.

Shiloh's gift is powerful. Her eyes do not simply look at you. They search through you, holding questions, answers, and simple truths all at once.

The room went still. The man shifted in his chair but could not look away. With no sound, no movement, not even the twitch of an ear, Shiloh spoke volumes. In an instant, she understood more about the man than he knew about himself.

The silence continued, and no one interrupted. It was as if everyone in the room could hear her thoughts and intentions.

At last, the interviewer reached for the stamp. His eyes never left hers. He pressed it down.

Approved.

Relief swept through the room. The older man shook his head, as if releasing himself from a spell.

We started to leave the hearing room, but Shiloh stayed behind, still watching the committee. Not with anger, but with pride. It was a sense of pride we shared with her.

Now they know.

Now we can tell everyone.

Thus confirmed as an author, or *pawthor*, and a true Canine Philosopher, Shiloh's voice now carries forward with authority and wonder.

We are proud to present the wisdom of Shiloh to readers everywhere, for this book, and for all the books yet to come.

\- The team at Corner Spot Press

Corner
Spot
Press

About the Pawthor

Shiloh is a perceptive Chocolate Labrador Retriever, Canine Philosopher, and a seeker of life's quiet truths. She notices things others overlook and finds wisdom in the small details of each day. Her reflections on animals and humans reveal simple, lasting lessons, because sometimes a dog sees the heart of things more clearly than anyone else.

Her mission is to inspire other dogs, and if a few humans learn along the way, that's even better. Above all, Shiloh believes every animal deserves love, respect, and a place to belong.

Prologue

I would like to take you on a journey, one that changed my life and might change yours.

My name is Shiloh. I am a Chocolate Labrador Retriever and a Canine Philosopher. I've always had a habit of sniffing out life's mysteries and looking for answers others might miss.

When I was a pup, the world was simple. It was all about belly rubs, chew toys, chasing balls, and learning how big and wonderful everything was. Every day felt like a game. Everything was new.

But in time, I began to realize that joy wasn't the whole story. Sometimes, a beloved friend would leave and never come back. A dog. A cat. Even a human. What remained was silence, sadness, and an ache I didn't understand.

So I began searching. Not by digging holes in the yard, but by digging for truth. I listened to stories, followed scents, recounted memories, and kept watch with curious eyes.

I had help along the way. My mentor was Henry, a wise Old English Sheepdog. Then there was Jax, the sly neighborhood cat. He enjoyed playing tricks, but turned out to be a lot smarter than I gave him credit for. And of course, Rocky, the Bulldog from the corner house, who taught me about persistence. He locks onto the mailman's leg and will not let go until someone makes him. I'm the same way with research. Once I grab hold of a mystery, I won't let go either.

In time, I discovered something unexpected and comforting.

There is a place we go to when our paws grow still. A place with no pain, no fear, and no goodbyes. Only peace, tail wags, and comfort that never fades.

I became determined to prove that such a place exists. I gathered stories, clues, dreams, and secrets only a dog can sense. Piece by piece, they formed a pathway to Heaven's Dog Door and beyond.

And now I want to share it all with you.

These pages hold the lessons I found about life, loss, and the bright future beyond goodbye. They also present a challenge: make a difference now and carry forward the happiness your best friend gave you before they left.

This amazing journey is not only about where we go. It is about what we leave behind, and how the spirit endures.

So turn the page. Let me show you what I discovered.

Because it's true... *Heaven Has a Dog Door.*

Act One: Goodbye is Only the Beginning

Silent Departures

I never heard them say goodbye, yet I still feel them close.
   —Shiloh

I first learned how quickly a friend could vanish when it happened to Milo. One morning Milo was there, trading barks and grumbles through the knothole in the fence like always. The next day he was gone. That was the start of a mystery I couldn't let go of.

What happened to Milo?

-Milo-

He was a mixed-breed bully dog, the proud boss of his back-yard. We watched each other through gaps in the boards, keeping score of squirrels and birds. He moved slower than usual, but his bark still snapped with authority. I thought nothing of it.

And then Milo was gone. No scent at the knothole. No grumble through the fence. Only silence.

By late afternoon Jax, the neighborhood cat, was perched on the fence, tail curled like a question mark. I barked half-heartedly. He blinked, licked a paw, and sauntered off as if the world hadn't changed.

Milo was nowhere to be found

Milo's humans cried. They said his name with shaky voices and stared out the window as if he might reappear.

I wished he would, too. But he never did.

I thought Milo's silence might be the only mystery I'd face, until later that summer when it happened again.

This time it was Lucy.

What was happening to my friends?

-Lucy-

Lucy ran so fast it looked like she was flying

Lucy was a little Terrier from the yellow house. She could run so fast her ears lifted like wings. She buried tennis balls in every corner of the yard as if she were storing treasure.

Sometimes Lucy barked at Jax to show off. Henry, the Old English Sheepdog, and I joined in from our own yards, while Jax pretended not to notice as he went along the fence line. Then Lucy vanished. No warning. No tail wag. I heard Billy and Charlotte crying in their yard, so something must have happened.

At first, I imagined she and Milo found a secret park, a place with cooler grass and slower squirrels. Maybe they were chasing dragonflies together or feasting on endless snacks.

But it felt different. Bigger. Heavier. Like a song that had stopped but still echoed in the silence. The air was still and lonely.

Even Jax kept away, as if his usual mischief would have been out of place. His bell stayed silent.

That's when I knew I needed answers, not just for Milo and Lucy, but for all of us.

I found Henry, the Old English Sheepdog, at the park with his human. He was my best friend and the wisest dog I knew. Ever since I was a naive pup, he'd been patiently teaching me the ropes about life.

"Here's how you get the best treats," was the first thing he taught me. Since then I have been under his watchful wing.

His fur was showing some gray, but that just added to his distinguished presence. I sat beside him.

"I don't get it," I said. "They just vanished."

Henry tilted his head, his voice gravelly, yet kind. "Yes, I remember that ache," he said. "When I was younger, I asked the same questions. I'll tell you what I've learned."

I leaned in, hanging on his every word.

Henry was my mentor

"When our bodies give out, our soul lives on," Henry said.

"We pass through Heaven's Dog Door. It's a quiet passage that opens when the time is right. On the other side it's warm and safe. The pain stays behind, but our spirit remains everywhere. Always."

The Dog Door? Other side? I tried to imagine it.

Henry didn't explain further. He gave me a long, gentle look, the kind that feels like a warm blanket and a paw on your shoulder. Then he walked away with his human, his tail swaying like a soft farewell.

I kept searching, asking, thinking, observing. I sniffed for answers in the wind, in dreams, in the places where paw prints had faded.

I even thought about asking Jax. That cat always turned up when things grew too quiet, as if he knew there was something worth investigating. What did he know that I didn't?

What did Jax know?

I thought of Milo's quiet fence, Lucy's flying ears, and the wisdom in Henry's eyes. Slowly, gently, I began to understand that something bigger was involved. The ache inside me softened. I still missed them, but I didn't feel so lost.

Maybe they hadn't disappeared at all.

Could it be they simply stepped through a door we cannot see?

When Paws Leave, Love Stays

The leash may be empty, but the bond remains unbroken.
—Shiloh

When a dog's final paw print fades from the path, the world doesn't feel the same. The toy basket stays full. The food bowl sits untouched. The air itself seems different, as if something warm and wonderful slipped quietly away.

I'd like to tell you about Einstein, because few know his whole story. Henry reminded me about it.

-Einstein-

Einstein was a big, shaggy dog who grew up with the Bradshaw family. He waited at the bus stop for the children every afternoon and kept guard over them as they played in the yard.

The children became adults, and Einstein stayed their loyal companion. When grandchildren came, he welcomed them with the same devotion.

Einstein waited for the school bus every day

As the years passed, Einstein showed his age. Every step was hard. The day finally arrived when pain outweighed joy. With his family gathered close, Einstein passed through the Dog Door to Heaven.

Now he is in a place where he is young again, bounding across fields, chasing squirrels that never tire, and resting beneath trees that are forever green. He still waits, only now it is for the friends he loved most to come find him again.

It is hard to understand because it feels so overwhelming and final. You keep expecting the jingle of a collar, the sigh during a nap, the gentle nudge that says, "I'd like to be beside you now."

But slowly, the heart learns. The spirit shows itself in the small things left behind: the blanket still carrying their scent, the sunlight on the floor where they used to nap, the smile that blooms when someone asks about your dog.

Henry appreciated how Einstein only knew kindness his whole life.

"That's how I want to go when my time comes," Henry said.

I gave him a playful nudge.

"Don't worry, old friend. You've still got a few squirrel chases left in that tail."

He growled in mock protest. Then we launched into a frolic dash across the park, chasing each other until we were exhausted.

Later I thought about what it means to miss your best friend.

Sometimes a memory flickers back in a photograph or in the way you pause near a place you once walked together.

Devotion lingers, even in a frame

When the time comes to pass through that gentle Dog Door, we do not take everything with us. We leave our spirit behind, tucked into everything we touched.

Take that special walk again, the one your dog knew by heart. The smells, the sounds, the rhythm of the path. If you listen, you may feel them by your side.

Einstein's family wasn't the only one to discover that love lingers after goodbye.

-Luna-

Luna was a small Chihuahua with a very big heart. She belonged to Beatrice, an older woman who lived alone. They were the perfect match and inseparable for many years.

Two hearts, one home

When Luna crossed through Heaven's Dog Door, Beatrice was devastated. She cried for days until, exhausted, she finally drifted into sleep. That night Luna came to her in a dream. She wagged her tail as if to say, I'll be waiting for you.

It felt so real that Beatrice woke, certain her little dog was safe.

I have heard about how humans grieve. They might cry while folding laundry or pause in the car because the empty seat where your dog always sat says too much to bear.

But in time, smiles return. Joy comes back. Your dog is still with you, carried in your heart.

Every time your faithful friend looks down from Heaven, they are saying, "I'm still with you. Always."

We are still wagging, just somewhere on the other side until we meet again.

When paws leave, love stays. And it always will.

When Our Human Crosses Over

Some say dogs don't understand loss, but we do. We just carry it differently. The sorrow lingers, and so does the bond.
   —Shiloh

Henry once told me, "We're only here for a short time. Our humans live much longer."

That thought stopped me cold.

People live longer than we do?

"But that's not what happened with Oreo," I said.

Henry lowered his shaggy head. "True. Some dogs lose their people first. It happens when the human they love with all their heart crosses over before them."

-Oreo-

Oreo was a small black-and-white Terrier with a nose for treats and a heart devoted to a kind man named Walter. Every morning they walked together. Every afternoon they napped in the same sunlit corner of the couch. They were a team.

Side by side, every day

Then, without warning, Walter died.

Oreo waited by the door, listening for footsteps that never came. Each creak in the house made him leap with hope, only to be met by silence.

Strangers drifted in and out for a while. Family members filled his bowl, clipped on his leash for a walk, but never stayed long. At night Oreo curled against Walter's pillow, ears at alert, listening for a voice he would never hear again.

On the third day they took him away from the only home he ever knew and brought him to the shelter. He trembled in the corner of the kennel, tail tucked, his small body shaking.

Then something changed.

Emily arrived. She was Walter's daughter, delayed but determined. When she heard Oreo had been taken to the shelter, she rushed to claim him. She could not bear the thought of her father's best friend ending up with strangers.

She brought Oreo home. Emily's house was warm and filled with life. There was a big yard and two caring children who gave him space at first, then slowly drew him back into joy. They didn't try to replace what he had lost. They simply stayed close. They talked around him. They let him know he wasn't alone.

Emily placed Walter's old flannel blanket in Oreo's bed. It smelled like home, and Oreo curled against it, though his eyes stayed watchful.

One of the children set a peanut butter treat beside him. He didn't take it, not right away, but he noticed.

Then, one quiet morning, Oreo nudged a tennis ball across the floor. The little girl rolled it back, and Oreo's tail gave a small wag. Just once. But it was a beginning.

Oreo's new family

Oreo showed renewed confidence. Soon he was running, playing, and curling at the children's feet with a sigh of belonging. He found a new family, but he never forgot Walter.

If you have ever loved a dog and worried about leaving them behind, there is something you can do. Make plans. Leave clear instructions. Choose the people you trust so your dog will be cared for if you cross over before they do.

Your pup may feel lost at first, but they will be loved again. And you will be watching the miracle unfold, the way Walter surely watched Oreo from above.

Henry was right. Sometimes it's the humans who cross over first, and their dogs are left behind to wait.

Devotion does not end at Heaven's Dog Door. It is carried forward until the day we meet again.

Heaven Has a Dog Door

I've heard it whispered in the breeze,
Of meadows past the sky,
Where faithful dogs find endless rest,
And humans grieve, then sigh.

But Heaven holds no gates or walls,
No golden palace floor.
It's open fields and gentle light,
And yes, a Dog-sized Door.

The doorway opens when we pass,
And silence fills the air.
We step into a field of light,
While our bond still lingers there.

No leashes here, no collars tight,
No ticking clocks or days.
Memories are everywhere,
They never fade away.

I wait, not lost, but listening,
For footsteps, soft and slow.
I'll run to greet you, as before,
With joy we used to know.

Heaven has a Dog Door, friend,
It's quiet, kind, and true.
And all it really means is this:
I'll always wait for you.

Act Two: Every Dog Deserves Forever

For Those Who Left Too Soon

Dogs don't measure years. We measure devotion.
— Shiloh

Henry, the Old English Sheepdog, told me once that some dogs never get a chance to say goodbye. Tragedy or sudden turns in life get in the way.

I wondered: how did they feel when they passed through Heaven's Dog Door? Did they still feel loved? Were they afraid?

Why are some dogs only here for a short time, a season, or just a moment?

These questions haunted me.

There are dogs who arrive full of energy and fun, wagging their tails and filling the air with laughter. Then, all at once, they are gone.

It didn't seem fair, and I couldn't make sense of it.

Henry could see I was troubled. After we played at the park, he sat quietly beside me and spoke about life's unpredictability.

-Noel, Buddy, and Bear-

Noel was a Poodle, Buddy a French Bulldog, and Bear a Golden Retriever. They were young, full of life, and deeply loved. They grew up together, side by side, adored by their family.

One afternoon, while the family was away, a fire broke out in a nearby canyon. The winds turned it into a wildfire, racing through the hills and filling the sky with smoke and flame. By the time it reached the house, there was no escape.

The fire ended their time on Earth, but not their bond.

Their bond was unbroken

Now they are in Heaven, still together, still playing, still watching over the ones who miss them. Their devotion did not vanish in the fire. It moved to a place where it can never be taken away.

For their humans, the silence left behind was crushing. Even the new house, rebuilt with care, felt too empty and still.

But their story leaves a truth worth remembering: rebuild your heart as you rebuild your life. Noel, Buddy, and Bear would want that. And they would cheer for the day new paws return to fill the silence with joy again.

There is another truth too: we cannot always predict tragedy, but we can prepare. Make sure neighbors know your dogs are home, and how they might help if disaster strikes. Check that sprinklers and smoke alarms are working. Small measures of care may one day make the difference between life and loss.

-Meadow-

Meadow's story was different, but her ending came too soon as well.

She was named after her favorite place, the wide field behind her house where she chased butterflies and rolled in tall grass. A lively Jack Russell mix, curious and cheerful, she always found something new to sniff.

One afternoon she slipped through a loose board in the fence. The road was close. The squeal of brakes filled the air, but the car could not stop in time.

Now, in Heaven's endless meadows, she chases butterflies once more, safe and free and never alone.

For Meadow, slipping through that fence one last time led her into danger, but it also opened into forever.

Her story also leaves a reminder: keep fences strong and secure. Walk your backyard as if you were seeing it through your dog's eyes. Patch every board, close every gap. Safety is another form of loyalty.

Meadow found the field that never ends

As Henry and I talked about Meadow, and Noel, Buddy, and Bear, a familiar snort and shuffle was heard drifting over from across the street.

Rocky, the Bulldog from the corner house, waddled up with his tongue lolling and eyes bright, like nothing in the world could slow him down. He smelled faintly of jasmine and adventure, which usually meant he had just finished canvassing the neighborhood.

Henry shook his head. "Where have you been this time, troublemaker?"

Rocky grinned, if bulldogs can grin, and gave Henry a knowing glance before trotting off as if we were just a stop on his usual patrol.

Rocky's burst of energy made Henry think of another dog who had once turned his strength into something heroic. It was an old friend of his named Maxwell.

-Maxwell-

Maxwell was a proud St. Bernard, a gentle giant with a faithful heart. His family took him everywhere: hiking, camping, exploring. He was their protector and constant shadow.

One summer day on a camping trip, two-year-old Kate wandered too close to the riverbank, lost her footing, and was swept into the rushing water.

Maxwell had been watching. The moment she cried out, he jumped into action.

The river roared. The water was cold and fast. Kate flailed, too small to fight the current. Maxwell dove in, his heavy coat dragging him down, but eventually he caught her shirt in his teeth. He pulled hard, but the river tore her from his grip.

He quickly fought his way to her again, seized her once more, and dragged her to shore. She was coughing, soaked, and frightened, but alive.

Maxwell's strength was gone. The river pulled him back, paws churning, body heaving. His family shouted as they nearly caught up. But he disappeared, claimed by the rapids.

Maxwell gave everything to save Kate

Now Maxwell walks a special path, recognized by every angel dog who sees him. He did not just live with dedication, he left with honor. And his story leaves us with a reminder: protecting your family also protects your dog. Maxwell gave everything to save Kate. But when humans guard themselves, they guard their dogs too.

Here is what I believe, with all my dog heart: every dog finds their place beyond Heaven's Dog Door, no matter how short their time was.

------◄O►------

Every moment in life matters. Every wag, every lick, every silly look, every lazy sprawl on the couch. We never know when it might end.

------◄O►------

Dogs who leave too soon are given back the time they missed. They run without pain. They nap in endless sunlight. They play, rest, and dream in a place where joy never ends.

And I am certain they know how much they were loved. If they did not get enough time to feel it here, they feel it now. Heaven makes sure of that.

They may have left too soon, but in our hearts, they are not gone. They only went through Heaven's Dog Door first.

A hero doesn't have to wear a cape.
Sometimes they just have paws.

Forgotten, But Not Forever

Some dogs never found their person on Earth. But that doesn't mean they weren't worthy. Heaven knows. Heaven remembers.
—Shiloh

What I learned really opened my eyes. I was walking through the park with Henry. He sniffed at a bush and moved on, while my thoughts grew heavier.

"A lot of dogs aren't as lucky as we are," I said.

Henry, we are very fortunate

Henry stopped, sat down, and motioned for me to join him.

"You're right, Shiloh," he said. "Some dogs wait their whole lives for someone to adopt them and love them. They survive on the streets, chasing scraps and shadows. They sit in shelters, watching the door for a savior to come"

He told me how some dogs flinch from kindness because it had never come before. They were never picked. Never petted. Never told they were a good dog, not even once.

Worse still, some are kept in dark places, left out in the cold, treated with punishment instead of compassion.

"What amazes me, Shiloh, is that they still cling to hope. Even the ones who are hurt or abandoned keep a small piece of hope tucked deep inside."

Henry paused and lowered his eyes. "They all wish for the same simple things: a warm place to sleep, a gentle hand, a name spoken with kindness. For too many of them, it never comes."

Then his voice dropped into a growl.

"There is a reckoning for cruelty", he said. "Those who are cruel cannot hide from what they've done. In the end, every truth finds its way back to them."

It startled me. This was a side of Henry I never saw before. My old friend had witnessed much in his time.

How can we let this happen?

This confirmed what I had begun to learn. I'd heard stories about these poor dogs. Henry had seen them.

I needed to believe that while their time may have ended, they were all right now. And I do. Because when they passed through the final Dog Door, Heaven was ready for them.

No cages. No cold nights. No fear.

Just softness. Just sunshine. Just tenderness.

For the first time, they are truly seen. They are greeted in Heaven with open arms, wagging tails, and more love than they ever dreamed of. They are met by other kind souls who have unlimited comfort to give. In Heaven, no dog goes unnoticed.

It doesn't matter how long they were here or how much they are forgotten. They are cherished now, and they are home.

-Lobo-

Lobo, a Rottweiler, never knew what it meant to be loved. Hunger was always there, and rough hands shaped him into a junkyard dog. The world only asked him to guard and growl, never to play or trust.

Abandoned on earth, embraced in Heaven

When his life ended, there was no gentle goodbye. No one whispered his name. He was tossed aside without the dignity every living soul deserves.

But Heaven was ready. In an instant, the weight he carried was gone, replaced by warm sunlight, soft grass, and arms that would never let go.

Lobo does not look down on Earth often, because there was nothing for him here but pain. But now he is safe. He knows freedom. And for the first time, he knows tenderness.

Here is what I know, and Henry confirmed it: the people who hurt Lobo will face the consequences one day. Cruelty always meets justice. They may have turned their backs on him, but Heaven never did.

-Cooper-

If you've ever lit a candle for the ones who no one claimed, whispered a prayer for the strays, or cried for a dog you never met, thank you. Dogs like Cooper feel that love, even from far away.

Cooper's life began well enough. But soon he was left in the backyard and forgotten. He found a way to escape and wandered into the city.

No one came looking for the Labrador mix. No one cared. He barely survived on the street. Hot summers left him panting

in the heat; winters were freezing. Injuries slowed him, and he hobbled as he searched for scraps.

One day, someone called a rescue team. They brought him to a clinic where healing hands treated his wounds and offered him food and comfort. The people there spoke to him softly, praising his strength and resilience.

But his body was too broken. He passed through Heaven's Dog Door soon after.

A little kindness meant the world

Now Cooper looks down with gratitude for those who helped him at the end. They comforted him. They gave him hope. And most of all, they gave him tenderness, if only for a little while. It meant everything.

To every shelter worker, every volunteer, every rescuer who reaches out in a desperate time of need: the dogs in Heaven give their love back to you a thousand-fold.

And here is what I ask on behalf of Cooper: if you see neglect or mistreatment, speak up. Report it. A beautiful life may depend on your voice.

God bless those who save our dogs

It was hard to discuss such things. I hoped the subject was over, but it was about to hit closer to home.

-Ranger-

While Henry and I rested in the shade of an old oak, Rocky the Bulldog appeared, dragging a branch three times his size. He plopped between us, chewing with gusto.

"We were just talking about how lucky we are," I told him, "and how some dogs aren't as fortunate."

Rocky paused, the branch still wedged in his jaws. "Like Ranger?"

Henry and I exchanged a glance. Ranger was the German Shepard who lived down the hill at the Filmore place. The yard was bare. The people there were not known for kindness.

"What about him?" Henry demanded.

Rocky shrugged. "He never has water. Hardly any food. He's always chained."

The branch dropped with a dull thud. None of us spoke. Rocky picked it up again and lumbered home, his stubby tail swinging as if he had said nothing unusual.

I watched him go, the weight of his words settling like a shadow over the grass. Some dogs leave too soon because no one stops what is hurting them.

Was Ranger in trouble?

Henry's voice was firm. "We should check on him."
And just like that, the decision was made.

We'll come back to Ranger's story. I promise you.

Second Chance Angels

Some dogs don't just find a home; they find a miracle. And when they cross over, they take that bond with them forever.
—Shiloh

There are dogs who stand at the edge of their time. In shelters, surrounded by the care of workers and volunteers, some dogs still see hope slip away when space runs out and days grow short. They come from many places for many reasons. Too often, they are overlooked, nearly out of chances.

Then someone sees them. Really sees them. And announces, "You're coming home with me."

-Jasper-

Jasper was a senior hound, half-deaf and stiff in the legs, sitting quietly in the back of the shelter. Most people passed without a glance. But not Angela. She knelt, met his tired eyes, and said, "You've still got time left. Let's make it count." And they did.

Jasper found peace with Angela

Jasper found a life of soft blankets, slow walks through the neighborhood, and naps by the fireplace. With renewed energy, he chased balls and rolled in the cool grass. On some days he looked younger than ever, a spark of joy reborn.

But time caught up. Walks became harder. His steps grew slower.

Every day still meant the world to Jasper. Every night he curled beside Angela, finally safe. When his time came, he slipped away peacefully, wrapped in warmth.

Another rescue came just in time, and his story still makes me smile.

-Baxter-

For Baxter, the Boxer with the great heart, the clock was literally ticking. He had only days left. His name was on the list no dog ever wants to be on.

Then Daniel appeared. A big man with a quiet voice and gentle eyes, he looked past Baxter's nervous pacing and graying muzzle. He brought him home.

Baxter came alive. He hiked with Daniel each week, barked at squirrels as if it were his calling, and somehow always managed to sneak onto the couch despite the rules.

Baxter found an extra life

Every afternoon after work, Baxter was waiting at the door, tail spinning, body trembling with joy. They walked together, then settled for the night. Baxter curled at Daniel's feet with a contented sigh, a shadow who refused to leave his side.

He showed gratitude in every little way. When he passed, it was with a grateful heart and a Boxer's steady snore.

But some rescues are harder, and none more so than Faith's.

-Faith-

She was a small Beagle with eyes that had seen too much. Born into an experimental facility, she spent her early years in fear. A number tattooed inside her ear marked her as property. Cold steel and cruel hands were all she knew.

When the laboratory closed, she was sent to a shelter. That is where Denise found her and brought her home.

Denise named her Faith because, as she said, "She's a fighter and never gave up."

At first, Faith trembled at every movement. She flinched from touch. But love is patient. Denise gave her time. Slowly, she began to trust. The first time she climbed into Denise's lap brought tears and a hundred joyful kisses.

Soon she discovered toys, all kinds of treats, and walks that made her skip around in excitement. She even joined other dogs at the park, something no one thought she'd ever dare.

Faith was never just a number again

For a few years more, Faith lived with kindness and care. When her body finally gave way, her spirit was unbroken. She left not as a number, but as a soul that was seen and cherished.

-What They Teach Us-

I have learned about many dogs like Jasper, Baxter, and Faith.

They were saved just in time, and they spent every moment afterward saying thank you in their own way.

Now that they have crossed through the Dog Door to Heaven, they do not look back in sadness. They look down with gratitude. Grateful for the second chance. For the rescue. For the destiny of finding them.

If you have rescued a dog, whether for years or for days, you became part of a miracle. You gave them the life they deserved. And now that they are on the other side, it is part of their soul.

-Can You Give a Dog a Second Chance?-

You can rescue a dog today

If you opened your home to a dog in need, thank you. You may not realize it, but you became their angel.

And if you find yourself wondering whether to rescue another, maybe the time is now.

Today, there are dogs waiting in shelters, foster homes, and rescue centers. The old ones. The frightened ones. The ones who have been through more than most. They still want to believe.

They deserve to feel safe. They deserve to be seen. They deserve forever.

If your heart is open, visit a shelter, adopt a new best friend, or simply share this story with someone who might be ready.

You do not have to save them all. Just the one meant for you.

The Ones Unseen

They came and went like whispered wind,
Too cold, too hungry, too worn, too thin.
No loving home, no steady hand,
Just fading pawprints on the land.

Some never felt a gentle touch,
And if they ate, it wasn't much.
No bed to curl, no ball to chase,
Only long nights, no soft safe place.

Yet still they hoped, with quiet grace,
For kindness in some hidden space.
A paw stretched out through rusted wire,
Eyes dimmed, yet hearts still full of fire.

And when their stories met the end,
With no one left to call them friend,
The heavens stirred, the Dog Door wide,
And love was waiting just inside.

Now they are held with gentle care,
In fields of peace and open air.
No more alone, no more afraid,
No shadows fall where love has stayed.

So if you weep for those who strayed,
Whose gentle hearts were once betrayed,
Take comfort now, their pain is past,
They're playing free, in light at last.

Act Three: All the Neverending Brightest Days

Staying With You

He took pictures of me sleeping upside down and doing all kinds of ridiculous things. I used to be embarrassed. Now I get it. Those are the best memories.

—Shiloh

If he only knew how many times I growled under my breath, especially as I turned away from his phone and refused to look at the camera. It was a game we played. I would glance just out of frame on purpose. He would laugh and try again.

Hamming it up for a photo is my specialty

I bet he took a million of them. Always with the camera, the phone, the "look here" voice. I didn't understand. I was right there. Why take a hundred pictures of a friend that never left his side?

Now I do understand. My search for what happens when dogs pass through Heaven's Dog Door opened my eyes.

Those photos? They are treasures: a tail wag frozen in time, a goofy blink at just the wrong moment, a muddy paw after a wild, happy day. They bring back the love, the laughter, the little things that meant everything. Those hilarious pictures turn out to be the best memories.

Some humans frame one or two favorites after their dog passes. Others make photo books or put our faces on mugs and cups.

I was at the park with Henry when he told me about the most photogenic dog he ever knew. I laughed and barked until I was hoarse. I thought I had heard it all.

-Charlie-

Charlie was the coolest, sharpest-looking dog in the neighborhood, and he knew it. A fun-loving Cavapoo, he carried himself like a star.

Shelly and George dressed him up and took him on walks through town. People joked that Charlie was more handsome than the men, and they tried to fix him up with their own dogs.

For Halloween, he was a pirate. For Christmas, an elf. All year long he wore costumes for the season.

Shelly and George even made a little studio in a spare room and took hundreds of pictures of Charlie. He sat still while they dressed him in every outfit they could imagine. Afterward they laughed together for hours, always with Charlie in the middle of the fun.

Charlie still shines like a star

When Charlie passed through the Dog Door to Heaven, they made a book with their favorite photos. It still sits on their coffee table. They even turned his best seasonal pictures into a yearly calendar so they could celebrate the joy he gave them.

-Sky-

When Sky, a Husky with eyes like blue crystal, crossed through the eternal Dog Door, her family wanted to celebrate her wonderful life by planting a tree. Not just any tree, but a young apple tree in the sunny corner of the yard where she used to nap.

It grew strong. And now, every year, it bears fruit that tastes all the sweeter.

Sky's family dedicated a tree in her honor

Others remember their best friend with their collars hung near a door or window. That is a beautiful thing too. It says, "You were here. You mattered. You are still part of this home."

There are many imaginative ways. It doesn't matter how small or creative, those mementos keep us close.

Henry and I brainstormed examples of what people do to remember. He shared even more.

-Simba-

Simba's story is a good one. He was a rowdy little Beagle mix with one ear straight up and the other flopping like a lazy pancake.

The perfect paw print

When he was young, his human mom made a pottery stone with his paw print pressed into the clay. She gently carved his name beneath it.

Years later, when Simba passed, she placed that stone next to his picture on the mantle. Visitors still ask about it. She always smiles and says, "He was the best boy."

Some humans keep journals filled with stories and dates, like the day we came home, or the first time we learned to sit. Some write letters to the dogs they lost. I think that is inspirational. We cannot write back, but trust me, we'll find ways to let you know we are fine.

Sometimes remembering grows into action, carrying a dog's spirit out into the world. They leave permanent, lasting marks of kindness as part of their legacy. Ginger is a great example.

-Ginger-

Ginger was a sweet, shy Golden Retriever who had a wonderful life. She lived with Beth, a kind woman who loved nothing more than sitting on the porch, sipping tea, and brushing Ginger's fur. Ginger would press her head gently against Beth's knee, as if to say, "This moment right here is everything."

After Ginger passed, Beth could not bring herself to sit in that spot for weeks. Then one day she picked up Ginger's old brush and placed it in a special wooden box, along with a favorite squeaky toy, and her collar.

But Beth went further. She started a donation drive in Ginger's name, collecting blankets and toys for the local animal shelter every winter. Her kindness ripples outward. Ginger's name is written in warm hearts now.

Ginger lives on through donations

None of these things change the fact that we are gone. But they remind you that we were here. That we mattered.

Some keep our dog tags on their keychains. Some wear necklaces with our names or paw prints. Some hang portraits. Some adopt another dog, not to replace us, but to carry forward the love we left behind.

However you choose to remember, do it your way. Loud or quiet, big or small, what matters is the heart behind it.

And when you look at that photo, or brush past that old collar, or whisper our name to the wind, I truly believe that in Heaven we feel it. We remember you too.

Remember on a Star

That one. The one that feels just right. I'll meet you there.
—Shiloh

So, that's what the sky is for

One summer evening, Henry and I lay in the grass beneath a sky of endless light. A million stars shimmered above us, scattered across the darkness like tiny lanterns that never burn out. The night was still. The grass was cool.

Henry broke the silence first.

"Some say that when a dog leaves this world, they become a star in the sky."

"A star?" I asked. "A dog becomes a star? That would mean there are a million dogs up there."

"Oh yes," Henry said. "There have been millions before us, and there will be millions after."

I shook my head. "How can the heavens hold them all?"

"It's not that we become stars exactly," Henry said. "It's that we create a little bit of light, and if you look for it, you will see that light again every night."

———— ◆◦◆ ————

So that is what the night sky is for, I thought. Choose one star, just one. Let it become yours, a meeting place for the heart where devotion still lives.

———— ◆◦◆ ————

Humans don't always know how to keep holding on after goodbye. Some let go too quickly, afraid of the ache. Others hold on too tightly, afraid to move forward. The sky lets you do both.

You can grieve and hope in the same breath. You can miss someone and still feel close to them.

It was no surprise to Henry and I when Rocky showed up. Not only did that resourceful Bulldog routinely get out of the yard, but he always sought us out. It was as if he could sniff something happening that he didn't want to miss.

Without a grumble or bark, he sat down and listened. He wore a distant look in his eyes while we talked about the stars.

Henry said he knew humans who stumbled on their star by accident. When they walked the same path they once did with their dog, they looked up and saw one star glimmer differently. Just enough to make them pause. Almost as if it saw them back.

That's how you know. You don't have to name it, chart it, or prove it. You just know.

And once you find it, you can return to the same place each night: the porch, the garden, the window at the top of the stairs. It becomes your meeting place.

The star may shift across the sky, as stars do, but if you go out at the same time, it will still be there waiting.

Some people use landmarks, and you can even write it down:

- Just above the roofline.

- To the left of the pine tree.

- Above the oak tree.

And if you forget where to look, that's all right. The star hasn't gone anywhere. It will always wait for you to find it again.

Dogs are good at waiting.

Rocky rolled onto his back, paws in the air, watching the sky with us. He was quiet for a long time, the kind of silence that makes you listen harder. Then he finally said, "I've never looked at the stars."

"I'm not surprised," said Henry.

"I think my mom is up there," Rocky added. Then in a whisper he said, "I can't wait to see her again."

There was a hushed moment. I thought of my mom too. Was she up there?

Rocky's mom is up there

Henry said that dogs are better at understanding the stars.

"We never wonder if they will be back tomorrow," he said. "Dogs just trust that the light will return, because it always does."

Like humans, dogs forget to notice the stars, so Rocky can't be blamed for not looking up. I know I can be so focused on pawing the grass or the smells in the park that I miss the splendid wonder above me.

Your star gives you a reason to gaze at the night sky.

If the ache of missing your friend feels too heavy, step outside. Let the night air rest around you. Find your favorite quiet spot.

The sky will open its arms and draw you in. Open your heart and look up.

Just like that, we'll be there.

The Star You Choose

When paws grow still and heartbeats fade,
And earthly bonds must part,
We leap beyond to Heaven's fields,
But not beyond your heart.

You may not see us by your side,
But lift your eyes instead.
We wander through the starlit skies,
Where angels gently tread.

Choose one bright star that calls your name,
The one that feels most true,
And know it's me within that light,
Forever watching you.

Each evening, when the night grows calm,
And all the sky is clear,
Look up and watch me wag again,
To show I'm still right here.

Though seasons turn and years may pass,
And night gives way to day,
The star you choose will always shine,
I'm never far away.

The Light That Follows

The stars bring comfort, but the sunrise brings a reason to begin again.
—Shiloh

Stars whisper, but the sunrise sings

Henry, Rocky, and I stayed awake all night, transfixed by the great sky of endless stars. I was yawning, ready to curl up like a newborn pup.

The air was cool. The horizon was undecided, dark on one side and glowing on the other.

"It's starting," Henry said.

I turned to see a whisper of color pushing against the night. It was a color with no name, one that made my heart beat faster and my tail wag without trying.

The stars were still there, but quiet now, as if they were bowing to something greater.

"Do you know what I love about a sunrise?" Henry asked.

I shook my head.

"It's proof that no matter how dark the night was or how long it lasts, light always returns."

I told him I couldn't remember ever being awake at sunrise, but in that moment I was glad I was.

"It's the greatest show on Earth," Henry said.

"Even better than the stars?"

"Yes, even better than the stars."

As spectacular as the sunrise looked, Henry reminded me it came with a bonus.

"You can feel it," he said. "The warmth. The sound of birds. The scent of fresh dew."

Rocky yawned. "I'm usually awake, but I never really thought about those things."

Henry and I shared a knowing look. Then he grew serious, his eyes on the rising light.

"Let me tell you a story," he said. "It's about a Labrador named Shadow, and how the sunrise saved her life."

-Shadow-

She was born into darkness.

Her name was Shadow, a Black Labrador Retriever with the softest coat and the gentlest soul. But she had never seen her mother's face, never glimpsed the trees that rose high above, never known the glow of the moon or the sparkle of a star.

Shadow was blind from the moment she was born.

Love doesn't need to see. It knows

At first, her world was warm and safe, guided by the heartbeat of her mother and the softness of her litter. But while her siblings opened their eyes and raced toward light, Shadow remained in darkness.

When the humans realized she was blind, their voices grew hushed.

"She'll never be adopted," one said. "What kind of life could she have?"

Shadow did not live in doubt. She found kindness in laughter, comfort in footsteps, love in the hands that fed her. Still, she waited for something she could not name.

Then, one early morning, it happened.

The porch was cool beneath her. The house was quiet. Her siblings were gone, adopted to other homes. She was the last one left. The humans whispered about decisions no pup should hear.

It was dawn, and the sky opened wide.

Shadow could not see the sunrise, but she felt it. The warmth. The shift in the air. The gentle breath of the earth rising into day. It brushed her face not as color or shape, but as life itself. She wagged her tail.

That was when the boy saw her.

Jordan sat on the porch steps, no more than ten years old, head bowed. His parents had brought him to meet the puppies days before, but he had chosen none. His smile had been lost since the accident that took his sister's life.

Now he looked up.

Shadow turned toward the warmth, toward the sunrise, and walked straight into his lap. No hesitation. No fear. Just trust.

And something broke open in Jordan. He wrapped his arms around her and did not let go.

"I want this one," he softly said.

That morning, the sunrise brought more than a new day. It brought a reason to be thankful.

That story made the moment so complete that I never imagined it could be interrupted. But then came a sound we all knew well. It was the distinctive clang of a tiny bell.

Out of the bushes, a black cat darted past.

"Jax!" Rocky barked.

Jax paused long enough to give a taunting meow, and with a whisk of his tail, he sped off.

Another day, another chase

It was the perfect beginning to an amazing day. The three of us jumped into action and the chase was on!

What I learned is that the sunrise is not just the start of a new day, it's the start of a new adventure. Isn't that what life is all about?

Every day is another opportunity to live life to the fullest.

All the Neverending Brightest Days

I recall the morning light,
That drifted soft across the floor.
The way I'd nudge to wake you up,
Then race you to the door.

The games we played, the walks we took,
The ball I chased with glee,
You laughed each time we raced the wind,
A joyful pack, you and me.

You let me bark at ghosts and birds,
And roll in summer shade.
You rubbed my ears, you shared your snacks,
Those joys will never fade.

The world was rich with belly rubs,
Of ball tosses, treats, and cheer.
But best of all were quiet nights,
Content in knowing you were near.

The clock hands turned, the seasons changed,
Yet joy refused to part.
For every moment shared with you,
Still beats within my heart.

So, if you wonder where I've gone,
Or question how our love still stays,
I'm running close beside you now,
In all the Neverending Brightest Days.

Act Four: A Glimpse of Heaven

All Who Belong

Heaven's bigger than I thought. Turns out, there's room for more than just dogs and humans. I know, it surprised me too.
—Shiloh

Jax has a way of vanishing and then reappearing like nothing happened. That's just how cats are. They can taunt a dog into barking, make them feel silly for it, and walk away without a care. Everyone knows about Jax and his tricks, especially Henry and me. Most days he slips off on his own errands, always returning with that devilish look in his eyes.

Jax was gone for too long

But this time Jax was gone much longer than usual.

The neighborhood started whispering. Tommy, the little human who adored Jax, taped a flyer to the mailbox and searched every bush on the block. The bell on Jax's collar was silent. Someone swore they heard a car screech late at night. Someone else claimed they saw a black shadow dart across the road and never return. Rumors move fast when the sun goes down.

I didn't believe any of it. Jax kept a schedule no clock could hold. He disappeared, collected secrets, then strolled back with that arrogant stare that says he knows something you don't. He never tells you where he's been, and he pretends you never asked.

I tracked him as best I could. There was a sharp cat scent along the fence line. Near the rose bush by the road, I found some black cat hair. Then, nothing.

Henry listened closely, his head tilted just enough to show I had his full attention. His ears lifted when I mentioned the cat hair.

"He could be on an adventure," he said. "But he's been gone too long for that."

We sat by the fence line, listening to the afternoon sounds. A blue jay whistled from a pine. A mower sputtered, then fell silent. The stillness that followed felt like a heavy blanket.

After a long pause Henry said, "Did you know Jax once had a sister?"

I turned my head. "No way."

"It was before your time. Her name was Destiny."

Jax once had a sister

-Destiny-

Picture a Calico cat with one white cheek and one orange cheek, balancing on the picket gate like a gymnast. That was Destiny. She didn't tease dogs the way Jax does. She loved sunlit spots, quiet corners, and mellow music drifting from the kitchen.

While Jax attached himself to little Tommy, Destiny clearly belonged to Tommy's grandmother, Agnes.

When Agnes grew ill, Destiny curled at the end of her blanket every afternoon. She would not move until the old woman woke and smiled. Then she'd hop down and follow Agnes to the window to watch sparrows. Destiny chased nothing. She guarded peace.

"Gone for some years now," Henry said. "For a little cat, she carried a lot of power. Quiet power."

I thought about that, about how a small life can fill a large space in someone's heart.

Henry's gaze drifted, as if another memory had trotted in from the field.

"Do you remember Wildfire?" he asked.

"The chestnut horse that lived way down on the farm road?"

Henry's tail thumped once. "That one."

-Wildfire-

Wildfire could run like the wind

Wildfire ran like the day would never end, his golden mane blazing like fire in the wind. He raced the school bus along the fence, tossing his head as if laughing. When the children climbed down off the bus, they rushed over with carrots and apples in hand. He nuzzled their fingers, then pranced and twirled in the grass while they laughed.

And he didn't just play with people. Wildfire sometimes cantered along the field where dogs chased one another, keeping pace not to win but to join. When they barked, he whinnied back, stomped his feet, and kept going. For those moments, he was as much a puppy as any of us.

"When Wildfire finally lay down for the last time," Henry said, "the farmer rested his forehead on his neck and thanked him. Some animals work. Wildfire worked too, but what people remember is how he made them feel when he ran."

I could see him in my mind, fast and free.

"And Michelangelo," Henry added with a spark in his eyes. "Don't forget him."

"The parrot?"

Henry barked a laugh and wagged his heavy tail.

-Michelangelo-

Michelangelo was a green-and-gold parrot who lived with Mrs. Alvarez on Rosewood Lane. He could mimic anything:

the mailman's "good morning," the squeal of bus brakes, even Mrs. Alvarez's laugh. When he barked like a terrier, half the neighborhood dogs went charging to her house.

Michelangelo was the star of the neighborhood

Every Saturday, Mrs. Alvarez wheeled his cage onto the porch so he could greet passersby. Sometimes polite, sometimes not, he collected phrases from the neighbors and flung them back in his own voice.

But Michelangelo had a tender side. When Mrs. Alvarez lost her husband, the parrot who never stopped talking fell silent.

Days passed. Then one afternoon, as she leaned close to his cage, he broke the silence with three words: "It's okay, love."

She wept into her hands, and Michelangelo pressed against the bars so she could scratch his head. After that he went back to making the street laugh. He wasn't a dog, but he was family.

Talking about him made me realize that companionship and belonging aren't reserved just for dogs.

Henry's eyes returned to me. "Destiny. Wildfire. Michelangelo. None were dogs, but each provided loyalty and affection, and each belonged."

It made sense. Heaven shouldn't just be for dogs and humans. It had to hold every creature who gave and received kindness in their own way, each with a place in Heaven to go to.

We sat in silence, the day thinning toward evening. Somewhere a screen door slammed.

I thought about Destiny's quiet courage, Wildfire's joyful runs, and Michelangelo's jokes. Then I worried about Jax, wherever he was, hoping he was just on another adventure.

My head felt heavy as I went home.

That night, when the porch light clicked off and the crickets sang, I curled into my bed and looked through the window at a thin slice of moon.

"If there's more to know," I whispered, "please show me."

Then I closed my eyes, their stories circling in my heart, and listened for an answer.

The Quiet Ask

The best inspiration comes when you don't think so much or push too hard. When you relax, answers magically flow.
—Shiloh

There was no answer that night, and my questions were wearing me thin. In every quiet moment, on walks or during naps, the same thought circled in my mind: How can I prove where we all go when it's time?

I was tired from overthinking

I would lie in the grass, watching clouds drift, trying to imagine it. Sometimes it felt close, almost within reach. Other times it seemed as far away as the moon.

Henry noticed, of course. He always did.

"You're walking like an old hound with sore paws," he said as we moved along the park path.

"I'm thinking," I replied. "It takes effort to wonder about forever."

Rocky, who was usually as oblivious as a puppy chasing his tail, overheard me.

"Whenever I get the urge to think, I just tear something to pieces," he said.

"Of course you do," Henry groaned.

Rocky wagged his tail, pleased with himself, as if it had been a compliment.

"But Shiloh's a Canine Philosopher," Henry added. "She's supposed to solve mysteries. She has a gift."

The words pressed on me like a weight. I felt an enormous pressure building, and something had to give.

That night, I whispered again: "Please show me. Please."

I stayed very still, listening as the night settled around me: the rustle of leaves, the creak of the porch, the slow rhythm of my own breath.

For once, I didn't chase after answers. I let them rest, as heavy as they were, and waited. The ache that was pressing against my ribs loosened, like a knot untying itself.

The sounds of the night grew softer. The air grew warmer. My paws felt light. For a moment I wondered if sleep was carrying me deeper than dreams had ever taken me.

And then... I was no longer in my bed.

I drifted upward through clouds, weightless, then touched down on grass so soft it felt as if the clouds themselves had settled beneath my feet. The air was alive with the fragrance of wildflowers and something even sweeter, something like home after a holiday feast.

A golden light moved with me, wrapping around my paws, guiding me forward.

I floated up through clouds and over fields

In the distance came the sound of barking. Some were familiar voices I knew well. Dog-like laughter followed, and then the rhythm of paws rushing toward me.

I was curious, yet calm. I was meant to be here.

At last, my quiet ask had been answered.

Through the Dog Door

The Dog Door to Heaven opened, and it didn't feel strange at all. It felt familiar.
—Shiloh

A Corgi with a halo was waiting for me

The meadow seemed to brighten as if it had been waiting for me, opening a path of welcome. In front of me stood a Dog

Door. Not a fence. Not a wall. Just a single flap that shimmered like warm sunlight.

A Corgi with a brilliant white halo waited beside it. Her coat gleamed gold and white. Her eyes were steady and kind, though a spark of mischief danced within them, not the troublesome sort, but the kind that keeps life interesting, as if she already knew more than she planned to tell.

"I am Hope," she said. "I have been sent to guide you."

"Why me?" I asked. "In my sleep, did I...?"

"Oh no, Shiloh." Hope's tail wagged playfully. "You are still very much alive."

I was relieved, though very curious about why I was chosen to be here.

"The One who watches over us sees your journey," Hope said. "What you learn will help others, especially ones with paws. The world needs a Canine Philosopher now more than ever."

Hope stepped to the flap and looked back. "Ready?"

I paused, knowing this was a moment I would carry forever. Then I nodded, and we went through together.

The flap brushed my ears like the gentle touch of a friend's paw. Warmth flowed through me, not hot, not heavy, just right. It was like the feeling that happens when someone you adore speaks your name. It settled deep within my chest and I felt at peace.

The meadow on the other side stretched wide. The ground felt like clouds and clover woven together. A gentle breeze carried scents I could not name, yet somehow knew. Dogs ran and rested. Some wrestled and tumbled into happy piles. Around each head glowed a soft halo, exactly like you would expect in Heaven.

Tiny lights drifted in the air above us. They winked and floated, never hurried, never still.

I tipped my head. "Fireflies?"

Hope sat beside me. "Sparks," she said. "When a dog is born, a twinkling particle, a piece of spirit appears here. It is the other half, waiting. From afar, it guides the pup toward good throughout its life, even when the world pulls the other way."

Sparks drifted in the air like fireflies

A Yellow Labrador Retriever trotted past, pausing as a spark floated near. When it brushed him, his halo brightened, as if bliss itself had found a home.

"When a dog's life on Earth ends," Hope said, "the soul returns here and reunites with its essence. That is when the halo appears. That is when they feel whole again."

I watched the Lab's calm, shining eyes and felt it in my bones. It was refreshing, like water when you are thirsty. I imagined the day my own spark would become my halo.

"And humans?" I asked.

———◦———

"Humans have sparks too," Hope said. "But Humans are given many choices. When they stay near kindness, their spark shines. Turn away too long, and it falls. A fallen soul becomes an ember. Fallen embers wait outside, longing to be kindled again."

———◦———

I thought of those who turned their back on kindness, like the humans who mistreated Lobo and Cooper. Their embers waited far below, longing for their counterpart to mend their ways and begin the steep climb upwards.

I also thought of my best friend, Henry, back on earth. He would be thrilled to know he was right about karma, and it just proves how wise and valuable he is to me.

Watching the Yellow Lab vanish into the meadow, I felt a quiet sense of closure, as if I had seen the end of one story and the gentle beginning of another.

Hope's tail swayed. "There is much to see, Shiloh. Follow me."

We walked at an easy pace. The air around us seemed to hum, not with sound but with a feeling that wrapped gently around my heart.

An Australian Shephard bounded past, barking with laughter in every stride. A small Dachshund with a brown and gray snout dozed in the sun, smiling in her sleep. Far off, a woman knelt to greet a Great Dane who leaned into her arms. All wore halos like crowns of purity.

I took it all in. This was true serenity: warm, fresh, and beautiful to behold.

My attention drifted back toward the sparks. "Do they ever get lost or burn out?"

"No," Hope said. "They can wait an eternity if they have to. They do not grow tired."

We climbed a rise as the view stretched even farther. I felt the pull to keep going and a rush to see what waited over every hill.

Hope read my thoughts. "There is no need to hurry," she said. "You will see what you need to see."

I sat for a moment, trying to take it all in. Who was I to be a witness to this place?

The atmosphere was remarkably tender, clean, and pure. I breathed deeply and settled my paws.

Somewhere a church bell rang, soft and soothing, but clear.

"That is a new arrival," Hope said. "Let me show you the first place they go to."

We started down a path together, paws light on the soft ground, sparks drifting above us like the stars I watched that night with Henry and Rocky.

Each spark carried a promise, and I knew that one of them was meant for me.

Forever Meadow and Lookdown Point

Perhaps the greatest gift of Heaven is looking down on the ones you love and knowing they are safe and sound.
— Shiloh

The grass changed beneath my paws. It grew deeper, springier, as if it wanted to run with me. Hope, my wonderful Corgi guide, smiled without showing teeth.

"This is **Forever Meadow**," she said. "When dogs arrive here they do not wish to leave for a while. They stay for as long as they want."

A bark rang out, bright and familiar. I froze, then spun toward the sound.

"Milo!"

He came at me in a joyful gallop, the way he used to race along our fence on Earth. We met with a thump of shoulders and a whirl of paws, tumbling and rolling as dogs do, laughing with our whole bodies. When we finally stood, tails wagging, Milo bumped my chest with his nose as if to say, *I knew you would find this place.*

I met Milo again in Forever Meadow

Then he asked about Jax and if he was still causing trouble.

"You know, I kind of miss that cat," Milo added.

I told him I was worried.

"As ornery as Jax is, I miss him too," I said. "He's been gone for a while, and everyone fears he's somewhere up here in his own part of Heaven."

Before I could say more, a little Terrier zipped past, ears high, tongue out.

"Lucy!" I barked.

She circled us twice, darted around our legs, then skidded to a stop. Then she tapped both our noses with her paw, very pleased with herself. I had only glimpsed her each day through the fence back home. Now I could see the whole of her: bright eyes, light steps, and a bundle of energy.

Here there were no fences to escape. Lucy could run anywhere, free and safe. She jumped up after drifting sparks as if they were butterflies, chasing joy itself.

We played a while longer, not to tire ourselves out but to feel the simple happiness of it. Hope waited nearby, content to let the meadow work its magic.

At last she tipped her head toward a rise in the distance. "There is a view I want to show you."

We walked until the ground sloped upward toward a glowing edge. The air grew thinner and a slight breeze brushed across my nose, as if we were nearing a great precipice. It was not a cliff, but the edge of a cloud.

Hope sat. Milo and Lucy settled beside me. Around us, other dogs gathered, gazing downward at a vast vision of people and places.

"This is **Lookdown Point**," Hope said. "Here you can see those on Earth who are important to you and the places that meant everything. You cannot change what happens there. You can only watch with kindness."

My heart pounded. I drew in a long breath and surveyed the view in complete astonishment. You could see everything, inside and outside. Even through the walls of homes where loved ones lived.

There was our street and my house, small and perfect, with a golden sun patch waiting on the kitchen floor. My human stood at the sink, then paused, as if listening. A moment later, he smiled and lifted his mug. The smile rose toward me like a balloon that did not need a string.

From Lookdown Point, we see our beautiful world

I searched the park. There was Henry, nose to the ground, patient as always. He found an old yellow hamburger wrapper near a bench and started to nose into it. His human arrived just in time and whisked it away. Henry sat back with a sigh, like a child being kept from stomping in a puddle. That Old English Sheepdog would never admit to scavenging for food scraps, and I made a note to remember it.

Then my eyes wandered until I saw Rocky in his own yard. A baseball glove lay in the grass, chewed and frayed, the leather hanging in strips from his mouth. His human shouted his name, voice rising. The Bulldog froze mid-bite with the guiltiest face a dog ever wore.

All around me at Lookdown Point was an endless pack of dogs, halos glowing, watching their people the way the moon keeps watch over the world. Among them I recognized Einstein, the St. Bernard. He watched the Bradshaw family set an extra bowl near the holiday table. The grandchildren laughed and played, more of them now than when he walked among them. Above the mantle hung a framed picture of the whole Bradshaw clan with Einstein seated proudly in the middle.

Something stung my eyes, not from sadness, but from the comfort of knowing those we love are safe.

"Do they know we're watching?" I asked.

"Sometimes," Hope said. "They know in the way a room seems warm and they sense a presence. They know when they feel something strange yet wonderful that they cannot describe, or when a memory arrives just when they need it."

The Corgi's eyes met mine.

"Even from Heaven, we find small ways to be heard."

Milo leaned against my shoulder. Lucy rested her chin on her paws. We stayed like that for a long while, looking. No hurry. No fear. Only the simple act of caring from a place that can oversee it all.

Above us, sparks drifted near the rise, as if joining us in our vigil. I tilted my head.

"Do the sparks look down too? Do they see their missing partners?"

"They wait," Hope said. "They are patient. When the time comes, they will meet the ones they belong to."

The Corgi stood. "It's time to move on. You'll have a chance to return to Lookdown Point someday. For now, let me show you the places that help new arrivals find their way around."

Milo gave me a playful nudge and promised he would be nearby. Lucy challenged me to a race later, which I knew she would win. But I realized, with quiet sadness, that it would be the last time I would see them for a long time.

I touched noses with both of them and felt the meadow rise beneath my paws like a continuous welcome.

Hope led me down a curving path between low hills. The light shifted in a friendly way, as though the path itself had a secret to share.

"Where are we going?" I asked.

"To the stations," she said. "They are simple. They are perfect. You will understand when you see them."

I was humbled to be here, astonished by the gift of seeing Heaven's path unfold before me.

We walked on, paws quiet against the soft ground, sparks floating above us every step of the way.

Heaven's Stations

In Heaven, every place feels like it is made just for you. Maybe that's because it really is.
— Shiloh

Hope led the way

I followed Hope, the little Corgi, along a winding path between low hills. The grass shifted from deep green to a soft, glowing gold. The halo above her head bobbed in time with her gait. Ahead, the land opened into a wide field lined with majestic trees.

"These are the stations," Hope said. "Each brings serenity and comfort in its own way. Every dog can visit them, any time."

The first was the far side of Forever Meadow. It was a different perspective of the same vast field that I first entered after passing through Heaven's Dog Door. I caught the faint scent of Milo and Lucy still playing in the far distance. Now I understood it better. It wasn't only a meadow. It was a thread woven through all of Heaven's splendor. That's why it was called Forever Meadow.

The ground was light beneath my paws. The horizon seemed to move with me. Dogs ran in great arcs, hardly slowing, never tiring. They went anywhere they wanted for as long as they wanted. A sudden urge filled my chest, the kind that makes you want to run forever too.

Next was **The Commons**, an open space shaded by tall willows and warmed by soft breezes. Dogs lounged there, some napping, some sharing stories, some waiting for reunions. It was a place for peace.

A puppy was lying on its back, soaking up belly rubs from every angel that passed by. Beneath a tree I recognized Cooper, who used to sleep with one eye open, always on guard as a stray. Now he curled soundly beside a new friend, a gentle poodle, safely at peace in a way he never knew in life.

Beyond the willows I saw **Squirrel Chase Park**. I laughed with a playful bark. Dozens of squirrels darted between trees, their tails flying. Dogs gave chase in bursts of joy but never caught them. The squirrels seemed to love the game as much as the dogs. One even paused, flicked its tail at me, then darted off again.

Paradise was full of squirrels to chase

I almost bolted after it, but stopped short. I had to be on my best behavior, here of all places. Hope saw my predicament and gave a Corgi-like laugh. I was a bit embarrassed.

We walked to **Cannonball Pond**. Dogs of all sizes leapt and splashed into its waters, sending up sparkling arcs that broke into rainbows. A Golden Retriever landed hard, water droplets glittering as it created a sizeable wave. Others floated lazily, eyes closed, peace drifting over them like the current.

Splashes of joy at Cannonball Pond

Along the shore, dogs were shaking it off, drying in the sun, and then running at full speed for another world record jump.

Further on lay **Echo Canyon**. The stone walls rose high, and every bark or howl came back layered, richer, as though answered by every friend you had ever loved.

Every friend you've known echoes back

I gave one sharp bark. It returned to me surrounded by other voices: Milo's familiar woof, Lucy's excited yip, and a deep, thunderous sound I did not recognize.

"That belongs to Maxwell," Hope said, smiling.

"I know his story," I replied. "Where is he?"

"You will see," she said, and I eagerly followed her lead.

Finally, we reached **Paw Print Path**. The trail glowed beneath us, stretching far into the distance. I looked down and saw my own prints appear, alongside small ones that I recognized as mine from when I was a pup. With unexpected delight, pieces of my life appeared with each step: the yard where I first chased a ball, the park where I met Henry, the kitchen floor where I waited for treats.

We went a great distance down the trail until the air became quiet. Dogs moved aside, making a wide lane in the middle.

From the far end came Maxwell, the great St. Bernard. His chest was deep, his eyes filled with strength and kindness. His steps were steady, proud, and unhurried.

"There he is," I said with a hushed bark. " Henry told me all about him. Maxwell jumped into a river and gave his life to pull a little girl named Kate to safety. She was only two years old."

"He is respected by everyone," Hope said.

Maxwell gave one strong, powerful bark, and its sound carried the weight of the river that took him.

Maxwell was a hero, even in Heaven

"Yes," Hope said. "Someday he will meet Kate again, at the **Great Gate**."

"The Great Gate?" I asked, with a pull rising in my chest.

Hope's eyes glimmered with knowing anticipation. The air seemed to have an electric charge around us as we moved onward.

We reached the end of the path, where the light leaned forward as if inviting us on. Hope paused, her gaze fixed far across the horizon.

I followed her eyes. There, beyond a rise, stood a gate, glowing so warmly that even from this distance I felt its welcome.

"That is the Great Gate," Hope said. "It is not for dogs. It is the way humans enter Heaven. The dogs you see near it are waiting for their person. Some reunions happen quickly. Others wait a very long time. But here, waiting does not feel heavy."

They wait by the Great Gate until their human arrives

Near the Gate, a small Chihuahua sat patiently, ears alert. Her tail wagged slow and steady, not in impatience, but in joy already blooming for what was to come.

"That is Luna," Hope said quietly. "She waits for her human, Beatrice."

"They adored each other," I said. "It will be wonderful to see."

"It won't be long," Hope added.

I looked again. Many dogs with halos were gathered there, all looking toward the Gate and the horizon beyond it.

"They don't mind staying for as long as it takes," Hope said. "When the human they cherish arrives, the Gate opens, and they meet again. That moment is worth every heartbeat."

"Why is it so far from the Dog Door?" I asked.

Hope's eyes gleamed with mischief, her tail wagging.

"Shiloh, there are many doors and gates in Heaven. Most living things have their own."

I thought of Henry's words when we talked about about Destiny, Wildfire, and Michelangelo. He was right.

"My best friend Henry once said, 'All of them deserve a place to go. All of them belong.'"

Hope leaned close, eyes shining, tail a blur.

"Everything that has a soul belongs. Even the great creatures of the sea have their gates. Whales, dolphins, and more. "

I stumbled back, wide-eyed. Hope gave a laughing growl.

"There's an ocean here?" I asked.

"Shiloh," she said, her eyes sparkling, "Heaven is extraordinary. Here, everything is possible if it involves kindness and compassion."

We began walking again. My paws felt lighter than ever.

I sensed we were nearing the end of my visit, and I was torn between staying and returning home. Would I have a choice?

Goodbye With Gratitude

Sometimes leaving is the hardest part, but it's easier when you know you can come back
— Shiloh

"It's not your time to be here, Shiloh. It was a pleasure to meet you, but there is more for you to do on the other side."

It was a truth I wasn't ready to hear.

How could I leave such happiness?

I was content here. My heart was full. I saw my friends, heard the stories of others, and felt a welcome unlike anything on Earth. There was nothing I could possibly want, except one thing.

"I would like to stay," I said.

Hope sat in front of me, her halo shining bright, her eyes alive with both wisdom and adventure. She wagged her tail.

"Do not worry, Shiloh. You will be back some day, and you'll see all of your friends, including me."

Before I could say anything more, sparks danced around me and then started to dim. The scent of clover and wildflowers faded. My legs wobbled. I was tumbling and falling, like when I rolled down the big hill as a pup.

Suddenly, everything stopped.

Slowly, the warm, inviting smell of home gradually filled the air. The faint tick of the pendulum clock grew louder.

I opened my eyes and woke up in my favorite place on the couch.

Peace filled my heart, and the light of Forever Meadow still glowed within. The morning sun spilled across the floor. From the kitchen came the familiar sound of my human brewing coffee.

I stretched and felt a burst of energy. I was filled with gratitude for everything that comes with living, and certain that someday my time would come to pass through Heaven's Dog Door for good.

I woke up with joy in my paws

I felt inspired. Something had clearly changed in me. Now that I traveled beyond the Dog Door to Heaven, I could never look at the world in quite the same way again.

And the first thing I wanted to do was to tell Henry.

Proof

When you've seen something wonderful, you want to share it with someone who will understand.
— Shiloh

My heart was racing from emotion and unbridled wonder.

I leapt out of the house and tore down the path to the park. Henry was in our usual spot, sniffing around the bushes like an old sentry on patrol.

I came back with more than a story

I barreled toward him, tail spinning like a pinwheel. "You won't believe it!" I barked. "I've been there! I saw everything!"

He turned to face me, his Old English Sheepdog eyes were calm, wise, and a little suspicious.

"Been where, Shiloh?"

I zoomed around, kicked up grass, and skidded to a breathless halt at his side. "Heaven! I saw Heaven's Dog Door!"

Henry studied me, quiet and still, as if listening for the truth beneath my bark.

I tried to steady myself. It was going to be hard to explain. Where do I start?

"Shiloh," he said calmly, "have you been snacking on chocolate? That stuff will kill you."

I didn't laugh. I couldn't. My heart still fluttered like dragonfly wings. "No," I said. "I'm serious."

Henry gave a long, shaggy sigh, the kind that comes from years of thought and even deeper naps. He lowered himself to the ground and crossed his paws. "Tell me."

So I did.

I told him everything, not just the sights but the feeling of it all. The way everything glowed. The warmth that came from everywhere and nowhere. Seeing Milo and Lucy. The poise of Maxwell. The joy of happy reunions, knowing old friends had never truly left. And about Hope, the little Corgi that showed me everything.

When I finished, Henry's ears tilted slightly. "It's a good story, Shiloh. But stories aren't the same as proof."

I thought for a moment, then gave my best dog grin.

"Remember being in the park? You found that old hamburger wrapper near the bench, and your human took it away before you could really get a good taste. You pouted like a puppy."

Henry froze. "How could you know that?"

"I saw it. From Lookdown Point."

For a long moment, he just looked at me. It was quite something to see him speechless.

Rocky heard us, lumbered over and sat listening.

"Big deal," the Bulldog interrupted. "A hamburger wrapper doesn't prove anything,"

"Really, Rocky? What about how you chewed up the baseball glove in the back yard? You got in big trouble for that, mister."

Chewed-Busted-Guilty

Rocky stared ahead with a transfixed look on his face, the same one he always wore when he was baffled.

Henry gave his tail an easy, deliberate wave.

"Well, Shiloh," he said, "maybe you really have been somewhere special after all."

If that wasn't exciting enough, the familiar soft clang of a tiny bell floated across the park.

We turned. Ten feet away, sitting in the grass, was that familiar, mischievous black cat. His tail was curled like a question mark, his yellow eyes steady on us. Jax was back!

Instead of chasing him, I wagged hard. Henry did too. Even Rocky wiggled his stumpy tail. We were all happy to see him. Our deepest fear was that he left us forever, and here he was, big as life.

Jax blinked, unimpressed, then stood and stretched.

We turned to head home, and that's when we heard it.

Out of nowhere, Jax surprised us all

"Silly dogs, don't you know cats have nine lives?"

We stopped. Looked at each other. Looked back.

"Did he just... *talk?!*"

All these years we chased him, let him mess with us, made fun of his attitude, and he was holding back the whole time.

Before we could interrogate him, Jax bounded away, climbed up a fence, and vanished toward Tommy's house.

We headed home, Henry, Rocky, and me, shaking our heads from all the amazing things the day brought.

Halfway down the street came the soft patter of paws, and Jax's jangling bell came up from behind. He slipped into step alongside us without a word.

That's when we all stopped being just neighbors and friends. We became a pack.

And even though my paws were firmly back on Earth, a part of me still carried the light of Forever Meadow.

Beyond the Dog Door

I've seen the light, I've breathed the air,
A place where love is everywhere.
Where tails still wag and friends still run,
Beneath a sky where love has won.

No fences rise, no shadows near,
Just every heart I hold most dear.
And though I cannot yet remain,
I know the path, its song's refrain.

So 'til the day I cross once more,
I'll guard the joy I'm waiting for.
For Heaven's real, I've touched its shore,
Love lives on, beyond Heaven's Dog Door.

DONA EIS REQUIEM
Grant them eternal rest

Act Five: Encore

A curtain call from Shiloh's heart to yours

Saving Ranger

The greatest rescue is the one you didn't plan.
—Shiloh

Remember when I promised to tell you about Ranger? Today's the day. And I'll warn you; it's not a story you'll forget.

Henry, our Old English Sheepdog, called a meeting at the dog park, and the four of us, Henry, Rocky, Jax, and me, gathered in our usual spots.

Henry was sprawled out under his favorite oak tree, worn out from a lumbering squirrel chase.

Rocky, the rowdy, big-hearted Bulldog, paced the fence line, looking for a loose board to chew.

I was in the middle of an important investigation, putting my Chocolate Lab nose to work and sniffing a patch of grass that held the week's best news.

And Jax, the ever curious black cat, was pawing at a bike left behind by a neighborhood kid. With one swipe, he sent the pedal spinning, the back tire whirring in lazy circles. He sat back, tail flicking, as if he'd uncovered some grand secret.

Rocky started things off, and it came out of nowhere.

"Ranger's still in trouble."

We froze. Even Jax's tail stopped mid-swish.

"Exactly what kind of trouble?" Henry asked.

"The kind you can't get out of alone," the Bulldog said. "No food. No water."

Henry looked at me. Days earlier, Rocky had hinted at this, but we thought he might be exaggerating. Rocky wasn't known for drawing thoughtful conclusions. But now we had no choice.

"We have to save Ranger," I said.

That was all it took. Five minutes later we headed down the road toward Ranger's place.

Bad house, bad feeling

The air felt wrong before we even arrived. The house sagged on its foundation, paint peeling in strips. The screen door dangled from one remaining hinge. Rusted car parts, an old tire, and pieces of trash littered the yard.

Inside, voices rose, sharp and angry. They were the kind that make a dog's fur rise.

Rocky led, and Henry and I followed close. Jax moved like a shadow somewhere out of sight.

We circled to the side fence, peering through knotholes. And there he was. Ranger, the German Shepherd.

Last time I'd seen him, he was strong and confident, with a bark like thunder. Now he lay chained to a post, ribs sharp beneath a shabby coat. The water bowl was dry and the food dish sat empty.

Every chain should be broken

Ranger didn't lift his head. He stayed motionless in the dirt, eyes half-closed. I was looking at a ghost of the dog he once was, his spirit dimmed almost to nothing.

Henry's voice was low. "We have to get him out. Now."

We found the gate, but the latch was on the inside.

"We're stuck," Henry muttered.

"Any ideas, Shiloh?"

"Rocky's jaws. Maybe he can tear a board loose..."

Click. The gate creaked open.

Jax was sitting on the other side of it, grooming his paw like it was no big deal to undo the latch.

"You're welcome," he meowed, without bothering to look at us.

We slipped inside. Up close, Ranger looked even worse. His tail gave a slow thump, and he was too weak to bark.

"Looks like we got here just in time," Henry said.

The chain around his neck was knotted tight to a post.

Rocky stepped forward. "I'll handle this. I'm an escape artist, remember?"

I once saw that Bulldog tear open a latched ice cooler. This was right in his wheelhouse. He grabbed the chain with his teeth, twisted and tugged it, and it slipped free.

"Come on, Ranger," I coaxed. "You need to run again."

He staggered to his paws, leaning into Henry for balance. Together we all slipped out the gate and down the back alley. Our hearts pounded with fear and the thrill of escaping.

"Run!" I barked.

I braced for the slam of a door, for heavy boots pounding after us.

We expected chasing and shouting, but no one even noticed he was gone. Sometimes the loudest silence is the kind that comes when no one cares.

Henry's house was only a few streets away. His human dad was in the yard when he saw us. He froze, then dropped to his knees beside Ranger.

"What happened to you?" he whispered, running his hand gently down his back. "Poor boy, come inside."

He gave the starving shepherd fresh water and a bowl of food. Ranger ate slowly, then curled into Henry's bed like it was the first safe place he had known.

Henry gladly let him have the bed and laid down on the floor. He would be the watchful sentry so that Ranger could sleep in peace. Rocky, Jax, and I were there too. None of us would let anything bad happen to our friend.

Henry's dad stood in the doorway. "I need to talk to his people," he said quietly. "But Ranger might have to go back."

The words shook us all and woke the shepherd up. Now we were too anxious to rest.

An hour later he returned. "Come on, Ranger. You have to come with me."

Henry and I locked eyes. We both knew what this meant.

Ranger moved slowly toward the car. Henry jumped in beside him. If the worst was going to happen, he was going too.

The car started off leaving the rest of us behind. I ran alongside until they pulled ahead, my paws pounding on the pavement, a tightness in my throat.

But they didn't stop at Ranger's house. They kept driving.

"In case you're wondering," Henry's dad said, glancing back at the dogs, "I called ahead to the pet hospital. Ranger's getting checked out and microchipped. He belongs to us now."

Ranger's rescue was like a howl in the wind

Henry later told me that, for the first time in his life, he was glad to go to the vet. The whole way there, he and Ranger stuck their heads out the window and howled like wild wolves. People turned to watch this loud, joyful spectacle of yelping dogs go by.

Just like that, we became a team: Henry, Rocky, Jax, Ranger, and me. A pack. Never letting go. Just like family.

Family isn't always the one you are born into. Sometimes it is the one that finds you when you need it most.

I knew then that the light beyond Heaven's Dog Door shines brightest when we carry it into this world.

One Heart

Five friends running side by side,
Tails held high, our hearts our guide.
Through fields, through time, we'll never part,
One pack, five friends, one beating heart.

Our story does not end. It was never meant to end. It simply opens into a new adventure for us all.

— Shiloh

From Shiloh, With Gratitude

Thank you for walking beside me on this journey. We've both learned, changed, and carried something precious forward. Memories stay close and strong, yet they aren't meant to hold us back. They light the path ahead in adventurous splendor. Wonder walks beside us with every step still waiting to be taken, and I'll meet you there, wherever your road leads.

From my paw to yours,

— *Shiloh, Canine Philosopher*